Spotlight on the 13 Colonies
Birth of a Nation

★ ★ ★ ★ ★ ★ ★ ★ ★ ★ ★ ★

THE COLONY OF
NEW
HAMPSHIRE

Dallas Yale

PowerKiDS
press™

NEW YORK

Published in 2016 by The Rosen Publishing Group, Inc.
29 East 21st Street, New York, NY 10010

Editor: Sarah Machajewski
Book Design: Andrea Davison-Bartolotta

Photo Credits: Cover, pp. 8–9, 15 North Wind Picture Archives; p. 4 Montreal Records Management & Archives/ Wikimedia Commons; p. 5 Boston Public Library/Wikimedia Commons; pp. 6–7 Maine State Archives/Wikimedia Commons; p. 11 Rainer Lesniewski/Shutterstock.com; p. 13 Snap Decision/Getty Images; p. 17 Fotosearch/ Stringer/Getty Images; p. 18 US Capitol/Wikimedia Commons; p. 19 DEA PICTURE LIBRARY/Getty Images; pp. 20–21 courtesy of Library of Congress; p. 22 VectorPic/Shutterstock.com.

Library of Congress Cataloging-in-Publication Data

Yale, Dallas.
The colony of New Hampshire / by Dallas Yale.
p. cm. — (Spotlight on the 13 colonies: Birth of a nation)
Includes index.
ISBN 978-1-4994-0526-2 (pbk.)
ISBN 978-1-4994-0527-9 (6 pack)
ISBN 978-1-4994-0529-3 (library binding)
1. New Hampshire — History — Colonial period, ca. 1600-1775 — Juvenile literature. 2. New Hampshire — History — 1775-1865 — Juvenile literature. I. Title.
F34.3 Y35 2015
974.2/02—d23

Manufactured in the United States of America

CPSIA Compliance Information: Batch #WS15PK: For further information contact Rosen Publishing, New York, New York at 1-800-237-9932.

Contents

Exploring New England

The United States as we know it began as 13 colonies owned by Britain. Throughout the 1600s and 1700s, the British crown claimed land in North America and set up colonies that were meant to earn money for Britain.

Parts of the land that is now New Hampshire were first occupied in 1623 as a fishing and trading settlement. Eventually, the colony became the ninth state, which made it the deciding factor in accepting the **Constitution** we still use today.

Although New Hampshire has a long colonial history, Native Americans occupied the land long before Europeans arrived. Two Algonquian-speaking tribes, the Pennacook and Abenaki, lived along New Hampshire's coast and throughout its lands. The first European to see New Hampshire was an Englishman named Martin Pring in 1603. He came in search of a plant called **sassafras**, but didn't find it.

an artist's drawing of the Abenaki

In 1614, Captain John Smith of Britain traveled north from Virginia toward present-day Canada to see if it would be a good place for a colony. He named the land "New England." Part of what he saw later became New Hampshire.

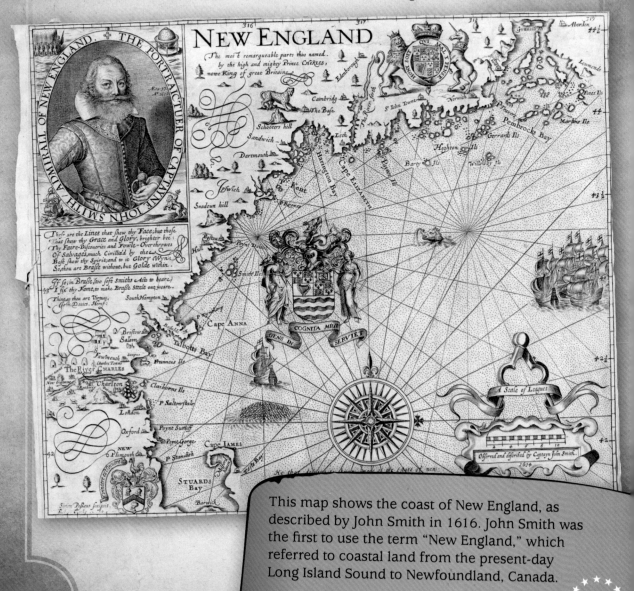

This map shows the coast of New England, as described by John Smith in 1616. John Smith was the first to use the term "New England," which referred to coastal land from the present-day Long Island Sound to Newfoundland, Canada.

Settling New Hampshire

Thanks to John Smith's reports, Britain learned the New England region was rich in **natural resources**. It seemed like a good area to settle. In the early 1620s, a group called the Council of New England gave land grants to Captain John Mason and another man, Sir Ferdinando Gorges. The land grants included the area that would become the colony of New Hampshire.

Mason himself never traveled to New England. Instead, he and several other businessmen sent two groups of men to establish a fishing and trading settlement on the land granted to him. The groups arrived in 1623. A group led by David Thomson settled near present-day Portsmouth. A group led by Edward Hilton and Thomas Hilton built a fishing settlement along the Piscataqua River, near present-day Dover. More settlements were built later, and the European population in New England began to grow.

In 1629, John Mason divided his land claims with Sir Ferdinando Gorges. Mason claimed the territory between the Piscataqua and the Merrimack Rivers. He named his territory New Hampshire after Hampshire County in Britain, where he lived.

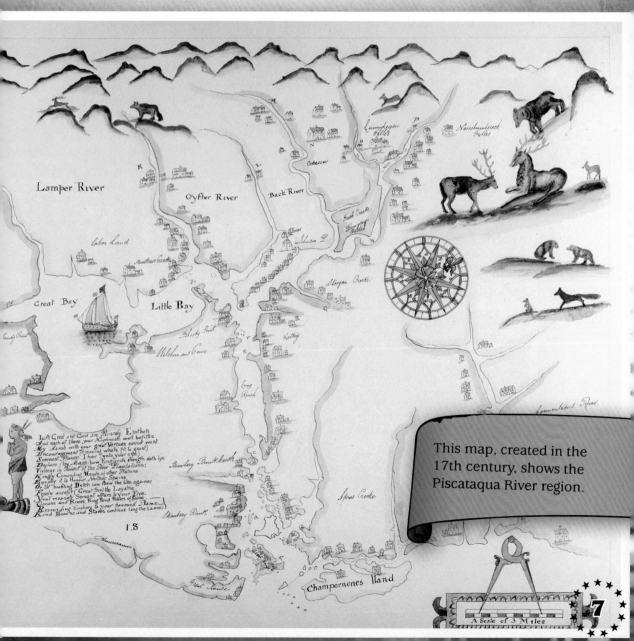

This map, created in the 17th century, shows the Piscataqua River region.

New Hampshire Grows

British settlers began arriving in New Hampshire shortly after John Mason proclaimed his territory. In 1630, he sent another group of British settlers to his land. Led by Captain Walter Neale, the group built a settlement near the mouth of the Piscataqua River. They named it Strawbery Banke because of the wild strawberries growing there. It was the first settlement to be considered a village in New Hampshire.

John Mason died in 1635 before he could see New Hampshire. He spent 22,000 **pounds** of his own money to clear land, build houses, and construct **defenses**. After his death, New Hampshire's communities continued to grow and flourish. British settlers built two additional settlements, Hampton and Exeter, and the fishing and trading industries became very strong.

In 1641, New Hampshire's communities came under the rule of the nearby Massachusetts Bay Colony. It remained that way until 1679, when Britain's King Charles II made it a separate royal **province**. He named John Cutt as its president. This only lasted for a short time. Over the years, New Hampshire switched back and forth between being ruled by Massachusetts and operating as a separate colony.

Strawbery Banke was later renamed Portsmouth. Today, Portsmouth is a major city in the state of New Hampshire.

New Hampshire and Massachusetts

In 1691, New Hampshire became a royal colony. Britain's rulers at the time, William and Mary, issued a **charter** that went into effect on May 14, 1692. Samuel Allen was the first governor of New Hampshire colony, but the Earl of Bellomont replaced him in 1699. Bellomont also was the governor of the Province of Massachusetts Bay.

A governor wasn't the only thing New Hampshire and Massachusetts shared. Some of New Hampshire's territory once belonged to Massachusetts. Many of New Hampshire's colonists had come from there. Massachusetts had a large population of **Puritans** who led a very stern life. Life in New Hampshire was less stern. People's different lifestyles led to disagreements over how the colonies should be run.

The practice of the colonies sharing a governor lasted until 1741. At that time, King George II established a border between New Hampshire and Massachusetts. The colonies were separate from then on. A man named Benning Wentworth became governor in 1741. He held the position until 1767. Wentworth was governor for longer than any other governor in the colonies.

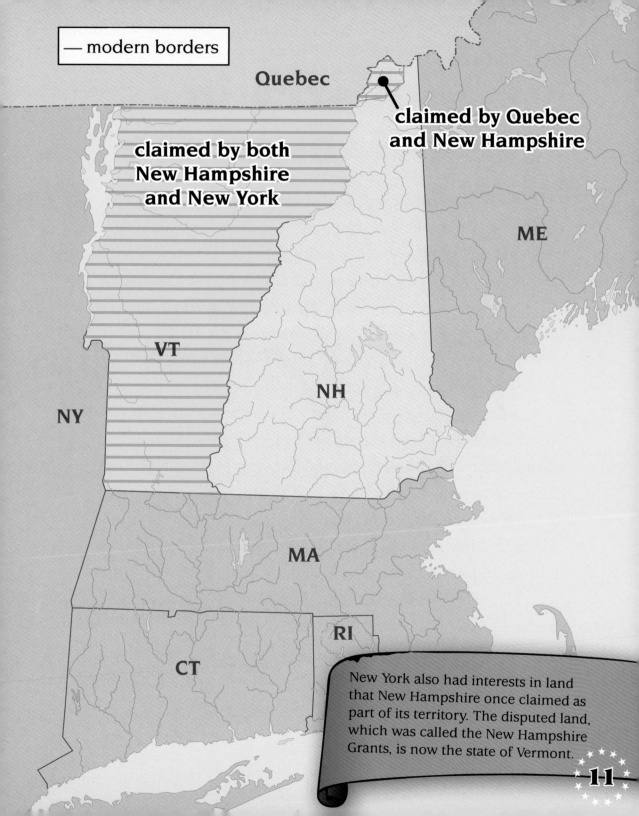

— modern borders

Quebec

claimed by Quebec
and New Hampshire

claimed by both
New Hampshire
and New York

ME

VT

NH

NY

MA

RI

CT

New York also had interests in land
that New Hampshire once claimed as
part of its territory. The disputed land,
which was called the New Hampshire
Grants, is now the state of Vermont.

Industry in New Hampshire

New Hampshire was settled and colonized because its natural resources offered many opportunities for Britain to make money. Fishing was the colony's main industry. New Hampshire's first settlements were built along the Piscataqua River for this reason. The Piscataqua River played an important role in making Portsmouth, which today is the state's capital, very successful. The city became an important place for businesses such as fishing and boat building.

Fur trading was also a major business in New Hampshire. New Hampshire's land was full of beavers and other small animals that were hunted for their fur. Trappers captured these animals and sent their fur back to Europe.

New Hampshire also had a big lumber industry. The colony was full of tall pine trees that were cut down and used to build ships and other products. All the products that came from New Hampshire—fish, fur, and lumber—were in high demand in Europe.

New Hampshire's successful industries helped the colony's population grow. By 1767, there were about 52,700 people living there.

New Hampshire was Britain's northernmost colony. Its geography gave it many natural resources that helped the colony become successful.

Rogers's Rangers

While New Hampshire's businesses were growing, Britain and France began to fight for control of land in North America. France owned land in present-day Canada, north of New Hampshire, as well as land west of Britain's 13 colonies. Britain wanted this land so it could expand its territory west. Fighting between the British and French broke out in what we now call the **French and Indian War**.

Britain relied on the colonies to help them fight this war. New Hampshire played a big role in the fight. Governor Benning Wentworth provided money and some of New Hampshire's best soldiers. Robert Rogers was one of them. He joined the British effort in the French and Indian War in 1755. Rogers was a good soldier and leader. He was asked to form a special military group called Rogers's Rangers, which was made of soldiers from New Hampshire. The rangers were good soldiers because they knew the land well. They were able to live in the wilderness and were good at fighting in heavily wooded areas. They helped Britain win the war.

Robert Rogers traveled to Portsmouth to find soldiers to join his rangers. Though the rangers were from New Hampshire, they mainly fought in New York.

Taxing the Colonists

The French and Indian War lasted from 1754 to 1763. Britain won thanks to the help of groups like Rogers's Rangers. However, the war was very expensive. Britain borrowed a lot of money and needed help paying it back. They also needed money to keep British troops in the colonies to maintain peace between colonists and Native Americans. Britain wanted colonists to help pay these costs. The British government decided to raise money by taxing them.

Britain taxed many goods, including tea, sugar, and cloth. The Stamp Act of 1765 was a tax on paper the colonists used. The Stamp Act made colonists very angry. Many protested. Colonists in Portsmouth protested by hanging dummies of the stamp sellers on trees. They even lit them on fire!

In 1765, John Wentworth, a man who became New Hampshire's governor a year later, was asked to describe what the Stamp Act was like for colonists. He said the tax made the colonists poor and unhappy. There was so much protest against the Stamp Act that Britain did away with it in 1766.

This artwork shows colonists protesting the Stamp Act with an effigy of a tax collector. An effigy is a model of a person that is meant to be destroyed or damaged, usually in anger.

Stamp Master in Effigy

17

A Revolution Begins

Britain's taxes and laws were meant to control colonists. One law that greatly affected New Hampshire was the Pine Tree Law. It said colonists couldn't cut down pine trees that were more than 12 inches (30.5 cm) in **diameter**, since those were reserved for the king. This harmed New Hampshire's building industry, and colonists were angry. Colonists in South Weare, New Hampshire, rioted against this law in 1772. This may have inspired a famous protest about a year later—the Boston Tea Party.

In 1773, colonists in Boston, Massachusetts, destroyed tea that was on board British ships in Boston Harbor. Britain's **Parliament** closed the harbor and passed laws to punish the colonists. Anger over this, and more, helped spread the idea of becoming an independent nation.

From September to October 1774, leaders from 12 colonies met to discuss their issues with Britain. New Hampshire's **delegates** were Nathaniel Folsom and John Sullivan. The delegates to the First Continental Congress (as the meetings are now called) sent a list of objections to Britain, which responded by sending troops to the colonies.

The First Continental Congress

When Boston Harbor was closed, British ships carrying tea sailed for Portsmouth. To show their support for Boston, New Hampshire colonists didn't allow these ships to unload tea in Portsmouth, and the ships were forced to leave.

The American Revolution

In December 1774, about 400 New Hampshire colonists seized Fort William and Mary in New Castle, New Hampshire, which was run by British troops. The colonists got rid of all the gunpowder and weapons inside the fort. This was one of the first military actions against Britain. Some historians say this was the first organized event of the American Revolution.

This image shows Fort William and Mary around 1705. The British flag in the right of the image tells everyone that the fort was British property.

The American Revolution officially began a few months later when fighting broke out at Lexington and Concord in Massachusetts in April 1775. New Hampshire didn't have any fighting on its soil, but it fully participated in the fight for independence. New Hampshire sent two generals to the Continental army, three **regiments** of soldiers, and hundreds of **militiamen**. Soldiers from New Hampshire fought in some of the war's most important battles: Bunker Hill, Saratoga, and Rhode Island. All these battles helped the Continental army win the war.

New Hampshire strongly supported independence. In 1776, it formed its own government. This government sent

delegates to a series of meetings now called the Second Continental Congress. It told its delegates to vote for independence. On July 4, 1776, the colonies declared their independence from Britain.

The Ninth State

The Continental army won the war when it beat the British at the Battle of Yorktown on October 19, 1781. The war officially ended in 1783, when Britain and the new United States signed the Treaty of Paris. The former colonies, now states, had to agree on how to govern themselves as one nation.

The United States first followed a set of laws called the Articles of Confederation, but this wasn't very successful. In 1787, leaders from each state met in Philadelphia to discuss this set of laws. Nicholas Gilman and John Langdon represented New Hampshire at these meetings, which are now known as the Constitutional Convention.

Instead of fixing the Articles of Confederation, the delegates decided to write a whole new set of laws, called the Constitution. In order for this new set of laws to pass, nine of the 13 states had to approve it. New Hampshire was the ninth state to **ratify** the Constitution, which made it the deciding vote in accepting the new laws. The Constitution is still used by the United States today.

Glossary

charter: A piece of writing from a king or other leader that grants or guarantees something.

constitution: The set of written laws of a government; also the written set of laws used by the United States.

defense: A way of guarding against an enemy.

delegate: A person sent to a meeting or convention to represent others.

diameter: The length of a line that passes from side to side through the center of a round object, such as a circle.

French and Indian War: A war between France and Great Britain that took place in North America from 1754 to 1763.

militiaman: A person who fights for a militia, or group of nonmilitary people who support an army when needed.

natural resource: Something in nature that people can use.

Parliament: The name of the United Kingdom's legislative branch, which includes the House of Commons and House of Lords.

pound: A form of money used by Britain.

province: An area of a country.

Puritan: A member of a group of British Protestants from the 16th and 17th centuries who wanted to reform the Church of England and who were also known for having strict moral beliefs.

ratify: To approve.

regiment: A military unit made up of smaller military units.

sassafras: A tree whose leaves and bark are used to make tea or flavor food and were used to treat sickness in the 1600s.

Index

Primary Source List

Page 4. Abenaki couple. Creator unknown. Watercolor. 18th century. Now kept in the Montreal Records Management & Archives, Montreal, Canada.

Page 5. Map of New England. Created by John Smith, engraved by Simon van der Passe, and published by James Reeve. Engraving. 1635. Now kept in the Norman B. Leventhal Map Center at the Boston Public Library, Boston, Massachusetts.

Page 15. *Robert Rogers. Commandeur der Americaner.* Published by G. N. Raspe, Nuremberg, Germany. Hand-colored etching. 1778.

Pages 20–21. *An explanation on the prospect draft of the Fort William and Mary on Piseatagua River in yr. province of New Hampshire on the continent of America.* Creator unknown. Ink and watercolor on paper. ca. 1705. Now kept at the Library of Congress Prints and Photographs Division, Washington, D.C.

Websites

Due to the changing nature of Internet links, PowerKids Press has developed an online list of websites related to the subject of this book. This site is updated regularly. Please use this link to access the list: www.powerkidslinks.com/s13c/newh